Mathematics 1

GW00726826

Add these sums of money. Write your answers on the lines.

a £6·43
£2·16
....

b £5·38
£2·24
....

c £3·49
£4·71
....

d £7·99
£1·20
....

e £9·24
£1·83
....

f £6·92
£5·27
....

g £8·99
£5·21
....

h £11·38
£10·99
....

Solve these problems. Write your answers on the dotted lines.

i The Biggs family ate a box of bananas in 9 days. They ate the same number each day. How many did they eat each day?

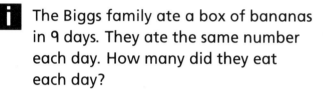

36 BANANAS

....

j Mr Small bought 5 boxes of bananas for his shop. How many bananas did he have for sale?

36 BANANAS

....

k Mr Long bought 4 boxes of apples for his shop. Then he made up bags with 6 apples in each bag. How many bags of apples did he have for sale?

30 APPLES

....

l Mandy was given a box of chocolates on her birthday. Her mother allowed Mandy to eat 3 chocolates each day. How many chocolates were left at the end of 2 weeks?

56 CHOCOLATES

....

Add the following numbers with tenths.

m 4·3
+ 3·8
....

n 6·2
+ 2·8
....

o 7·7
+ 3·5
....

p 9·6
+ 4·5
....

q 8·8
+ 7·7
....

Subtract the following numbers with tenths.

r 9·4
– 7·6
....

s 8·3
– 6·5
....

t 10·3
– 8·4
....

u 16·8
– 6·9
....

v 20·1
– 9·4
....

Use this extract from a dictionary to answer the questions below.

tardy	slow or late	**tinge**	to colour slightly
taunt	a jeering or mocking remark	**token**	a sign
taut	pulled tightly	**topaz**	a precious stone
tawdry	showy, but cheap and common	**torrid**	very hot
teak	a hard, long-lasting timber	**tranquil**	quiet and peaceful
tempest	a violent storm	**transmit**	to send or pass on
tepid	lukewarm	**traverse**	to go across
textile	a woven material	**tremor**	a trembling or vibration
thong	a long narrow strip of leather	**trio**	a group of three musicians or persons
throng	a crowd	**trivial**	of little value or importance
76		77	

a Could you boil an egg in **tepid** water? _____

b Is a **topaz** worth a lot of money? _____

c Is **teak** a soft or hard wood? _____

d Does slack mean the opposite of **taut**? _____

e Which of the two words in brackets fits into this sentence? [thong, throng]

"A great _____ of people gathered in the town square."

f Which would you feel in an earthquake, a **tremor** or a **tranquil**? _____

g Which would you wear, **torrid** or **textile**? _____

h Which would you rather be, **trivial** or **tranquil**? _____

i Can aircraft **traverse** the Atlantic Ocean? _____

j Which word listed fits into this sentence?
"The day was too _____ for running a marathon."

k Which of these could do damage? [tempest, token] _____

A pronoun is a word used instead of a noun. Put a ring round each pronoun and underline every noun in the following.

l Tania decided to plant a tree in her garden. She dug a hole and put manure in it. Then she poured some water in the hole. She placed the tree in the hole and made sure it was straight. Then she filled in the hole with soil and firmed it down with her foot.

Science 1

After each sentence there are two words.

Write the correct word to complete the sentence.

a To work and play the human body needs
_____ . [energy, exert]

b The human body is like a _____ .
[engine, machine]

c But it can do things that no _____
can do. [doctor, machine]

d It can _____ . [grow, stop]

e It can _____ itself. [report, repair]

f _____ heal and broken bones join
together. [Wounds, Hairs]

g The human body gets energy from
_____ and drink. [food, work]

h Also, our bodies need _____ . [clothes, air]

i The _____ in the air helps to break down food so that it can be
used as energy. [hydrogen, oxygen]

j The human _____ is like a battery. [body, brain]

k Like a battery, it runs _____ and has to be recharged. [up, down]

l _____ people need more sleep than adults. [Young, Tired]

m That is because they are still _____ . [growing, young]

n So, the human body needs _____ , drink, air and sleep.
[play, food]

o Without these _____ things we would die. [five, four]

Writing 1

This sentence is in the **present tense:**   Jack *is* watching a video.
This sentence is in the **past tense:**   Jack *was* watching a video.

Write these sentences in the past tense.

a Peter is peeling potatoes for dinner.

_____

b The four girls are playing tennis.

_____

c Tim and Chris have homework to do.

_____

d It is Autumn and the leaves are falling.

_____

The apostrophe is used in the place of letters that have been left out of words to make contractions.

"Let's *(let us)* pretend you're *(you are)* a pop star.
I'll *(I will)* ask you questions, and you'll *(you will)* answer them."

Write the following interview, putting in apostrophes where they are needed.

e Wed all the bad luck, thats for sure. Shouldve scored
at least three in the first half – four if the referee
hadnt got in the way. And theres that penalty. Dont
tell me the keeper didnt move before the ball was
struck. Theyd all the luck in the second half. Ive never
seen the like! Things just werent going for us. Wasnt
our day. Four of the goals shouldnt have been
allowed. Anyway, thats what I think. Were all
shattered. But well beat em next time, dont you worry.

_____

_____

_____

_____

_____

_____

_____

_____

Schofield&Sims **Homework 4 Photocopiable Edition**

Thinking 1

a Begin at any letter and follow the lines to spell the name of a sport. You must not skip letters.
Spell the names of six sports.

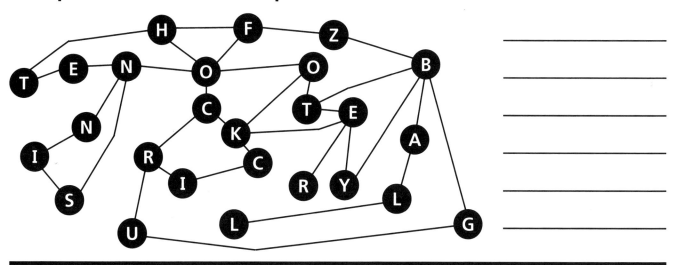

_____

_____

_____

_____

_____

_____

Fill in the blanks.

b 2 4 8 ___ 32 ___

c 3 6 ___ 24 ___ 96

d £1 ___ 20p 10p ___ 2p 1p

e 75p £1·50 £3 ___

f
| 1:45 | 2:15 | 2:45 | | 3:45 | |

g Write the following dates in their correct order in the year.

2 April   _____

4 November   _____

23 September   _____

28 February   _____

30 March   _____

16 July   _____

6 November   _____

3 October   _____

6 June   _____

1 February   _____

Reading and Vocabulary 2

Read the passage and answer the questions.

People from the same race are alike in many ways. But they are also different in many ways. Brothers and sisters, and even twins are not quite the same. You are different from everyone else in the world. There is only one of you.

All human beings come from the same ancestors. So, all the people of the world are related. People who have lived for a long time in different parts of the world have changed and altered in a number of ways. Different races of people have different-coloured skins. People from hot parts of Africa have dark skins. This protects their skin from sunburn. Many Africans have dark eyes which help them to see better in bright sunlight.

People who come from places where there is not much sunlight have light-coloured skins. This helps their bodies to make the most of the sunlight they do get. Europeans have the lightest skins.

a Do all human beings come from the same ancestors? _____

b What word describes the skin of people from hot parts of Africa? _____

c What does a dark skin protect people from? _____

d In which race do many of the people have dark skin? _____

e Which race of people have the lightest skins? _____

f Are twins exactly alike? _____

Underline the odd word out in each line.

g	amazing	surprising	ordinary	astounding	astonishing
h	usual	seldom	regular	normal	constant
i	request	order	command	rule	control
j	splendid	glorious	brilliant	delightful	gigantic
k	weary	tired	relaxed	listless	fatigued

Schofield & Sims **Homework 4 Photocopiable Edition**

Mathematics 2

Write the fractions that are shaded and not shaded in each shape.
The first one is done for you.

a
$\frac{3}{4}$ shaded
$\frac{1}{4}$ not shaded

b
shaded
not shaded

c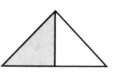
shaded
not shaded

d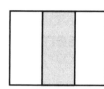
shaded
not shaded

e
shaded
not shaded

f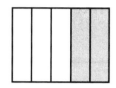
shaded
not shaded

g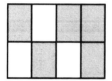
shaded
not shaded

h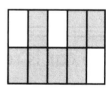
shaded
not shaded

Write the answers to these division sums above the line.
The first one is done for you.

i $3\overline{)9}$ = 3   **j** $3\overline{)21}$ **k** $5\overline{)40}$ **l** $4\overline{)36}$ **m** $8\overline{)32}$

n $3\overline{)36}$ **o** $5\overline{)45}$ **p** $4\overline{)28}$ **q** $7\overline{)49}$ **r** $8\overline{)64}$

Write your answer to each multiplication sum on the dotted line.

s
$$\begin{array}{r} 15 \\ \times\ 7 \\ \hline \end{array}$$

t
$$\begin{array}{r} 19 \\ \times\ 3 \\ \hline \end{array}$$

u
$$\begin{array}{r} 36 \\ \times\ 5 \\ \hline \end{array}$$

v
$$\begin{array}{r} 38 \\ \times\ 6 \\ \hline \end{array}$$

w
$$\begin{array}{r} 45 \\ \times\ 4 \\ \hline \end{array}$$

x
$$\begin{array}{r} 53 \\ \times\ 8 \\ \hline \end{array}$$

y
$$\begin{array}{r} 72 \\ \times\ 5 \\ \hline \end{array}$$

z
$$\begin{array}{r} 94 \\ \times\ 9 \\ \hline \end{array}$$

Language Skills 2

A prefix added to a word can change the meaning of the word: for example happy ➡ <u>un</u>happy.

Add a prefix to one word in each sentence to change the meaning.

a It is possible to climb this cliff.

_____

b There is a lot of sense in this book.

_____

c Terry says he likes cabbage.

_____

d The answer you gave me is correct.

_____

e The price of the car is reasonable.

_____

A verb is a word that tells what is done or what exists.
For example, Nina <u>found</u> a stray cat and <u>fed</u> it.

Underline the verbs in the following.

f The snow fell all night. When Melvin opened the front door, the wind blew the snow into the hall.

After breakfast Melvin and Pearl dragged their sledge to the top of the hill. They sat on it, and it slid down the slope at high speed.

But they had forgotten the stream at the foot of the hill. The sledge plunged into it. The two children were thrown into the water. They scrambled out, shivering and with their teeth chattering.

Science 2

Use a word from this list to fill each blank.

small	pieces	eat	used	mouth
swallow	energy	mixed	body	stomach
food	large	teeth	waste	juices

The food we _____ has to be broken down so that it can be used by all parts of the body. We take food into our _____ . We chew it with our grinding _____ . A liquid called saliva mixes with our _____ . The saliva makes the food easy to _____ . The food goes down a tube to the _____ . In the stomach other _____ mix with the food. When it is almost a liquid, the food goes into the _____ intestine. There it is _____ with other juices. Then it is ready to be used in all parts of the_____ .
The food has been made into tiny _____ . It goes into the blood and is used as _____ in all parts of the body. Some of the food cannot be _____ by the body.
This _____ food passes through the _____ intestine and out of the body.

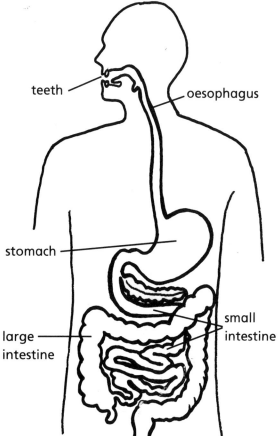

teeth

oesophagus

stomach

large intestine

small intestine

Writing 2

These sentences are in the past tense.
Write them in the present tense.

a Harry was playing with a toy crane.

_____

b The girls were making costumes for the play.

_____

c Sara and Owen had measles.

_____

d It was Spring and the trees were in bud.

_____

e They could not find the lost ball in the bushes.

_____

In the following sentence, the comma is used to show a short pause.

I love ice-cream, especially raspberry flavour.

Write out the following passage, putting in commas for pauses where they are needed.

f Thousands of years ago there was no money. Instead people traded by exchanging goods. Later people began using different kinds of money like shells and flat stones with holes in them.

Some of these strange coins as in the South Sea Islands were as much as three metres across. Then in time people began to make money. Metal which had always been considered valuable lasted much longer. The Greeks were the first to make silver coins with heads and symbols on them very like the coins of today.

_____

_____

_____

_____

_____

_____

Mr and Mrs Hicks had four children: Jack, Joe, Julie and Jane. Jane married and had three children: Freddie, Helen and Grant. Then Joe married and he and his wife had two children, Andrew and Samantha.

How many of each of the following had Samantha?

a uncles ☐　　　**b** aunts ☐　　　**c** cousins ☐

These pictures are in the wrong order.
Write the number of the pictures in their correct order.

d
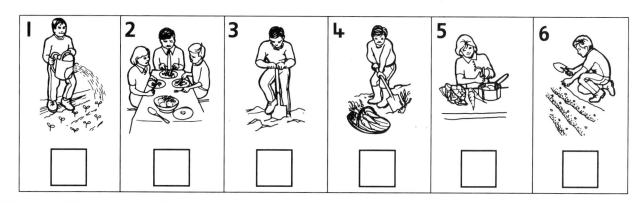

Write the word that does not belong.

e carrot, potato, plum, cabbage, beans　　　_____

f hammer, saw, screwdriver, bench, pliers　　　_____

g mean, kind, nasty, spiteful, base　　　_____

h keep, protect, guard, detain, release　　　_____

i scissors, screw, nail, gum, glue　　　_____

j end, final, last, next, concluding　　　_____

k chicken, shark, cheap, cheer, cheese　　　_____

l brittle, fragile, slim, frail, delicate　　　_____

Reading and Vocabulary 3

Read the passage. Where there are two words in brackets, cross out the word that does not fit, and leave the word that makes sense in the sentence.

There **[will/was]** a man who had five sons. These sons **[were/was]** always quarrelling **[along/among]** themselves. Their father decided to show them how **[silly/sensible]** they were. He collected five sticks, each the same length, and tied them **[apart/together]**. Then he said to his sons, "Listen to me! Break this bundle of sticks over your **[shoulder/knee]**."

"Easy!" said the eldest **[son/child]**. He took the bundle and **[threw/pulled]** it against his knee with all his **[arms/strength]**. But he could not **[break/undo]** the five sticks in the bundle. Then each brother in turn tried, but the bundle remained **[tied/unbroken]**.

"Let me show you," said their father, "how it can be **[done/undone]**." He **[tied/untied]** the rope which held the sticks together. Then he handed one stick to each of his **[four/five]** sons. "Now," he ordered, "each of you break the **[stick/bundle]** in your hands." The sons did so. Each stick **[held/cracked]** easily. "What do you **[want/make]** of that?" their father asked them.

His sons looked **[puzzled/pleased]**, and made no answer. Their father **[cried/sighed]**.

"Don't you see?" he **[shouted/explained]** patiently. "When a man stands **[together/alone]**, he can be broken as easily as **[one/five]** of those sticks. But when a man stands **[united/alone]** with others, nothing can break him."

Then the sons **[misunderstood/understood]** what their father had been trying to tell them. They became **[nervous/ashamed]** of the quarrelling they had done. The eldest son said, "I see – **[divided/united]** we stand, divided we fall."

HOMEWORK BOOK 4 ANSWERS

Note for users

Taking an interest in the child's work is of great importance. Take every opportunity to praise work that is correct, and offer help and advice where the child experiences difficulty. Make sure that the child understands the instructions which introduce each exercise. Some children experience more difficulty with the instructions than with the work itself.

There are advantages in allowing the child to mark his or her own work. This informs the child of the correct answer in cases where mistakes have occurred. It is important to look again at answers that are wrong and for the child to discover why an answer is incorrect so that he or she can learn as a result of the error.

Where a weakness is revealed, further similar exercises can be provided to give the child more practice and confidence.

A child should not be expected to undertake too much work in a short time. The exercises should be well spaced out so that the last pages are being worked towards the end of the appropriate school year.

Schofield & Sims Homework 4 Photocopiable Edition

Reading and Vocabulary 1

a yes
b ice and dust
c the tail
d gas and dust
e no
f yes
g yes
h repeat
i inhale
j decide
k moult
l starve
m regrets

 Mathematics 1

a £8·59
b £7·62
c £8·20
d £9·19
e £11·07
f £12·19
g £14·20
h £22·37
i 4
j 180
k 20
l 14
m 8.1
n 9.0
o 11.2
p 14.1
q 16.5
r 1.8
s 1.8
t 1.9
u 9.9
v 10.7

 Language Skills 1

a no
b yes
c hard
d yes
e throng
f tremor
g textile
h tranquil
i yes
j torrid
k tempest

l *Nouns:* <u>Tania</u> <u>tree</u> <u>garden</u> <u>hole</u> <u>manure</u> <u>water</u> <u>hole</u> <u>tree</u> <u>hole</u> <u>hole</u> <u>soil</u> <u>foot</u>

Pronouns: her She it She she it she it her

 Science 1

a energy
b machine
c machine
d grow
e repair
f Wounds
g food
h air
i oxygen
j body
k down
l Young
m growing
n food
o four

 Writing 1

a Peter was peeling potatoes for dinner.
b The four girls were playing tennis.
c Tim and Chris had homework to do.
d It was Autumn and the leaves were falling.

e We'd all the bad luck, that's for sure. Should've scored at least three in the first half – four if the referee hadn't got in the way. And there's that penalty. Don't tell me the keeper didn't move before the ball was struck. They'd all the luck in the second half. I've never seen the like! Things just weren't going for us. Wasn't our day. Four of the goals shouldn't have been allowed. Anyway, that's what I think. We're all shattered. But we'll beat 'em next time, don't you worry.

 Thinking 1

a tennis, snooker, hockey, cricket, football, rugby
b 16, 64
c 12, 48
d 50p, 5p
e £6
f 3:15, 4:15
g 1 February, 28 February, 30 March, 2 April, 6 June, 16 July, 23 September, 3 October, 4 November, 6 November

 Reading and Vocabulary 2

a yes
b dark
c sunburn
d Africans
e Europeans
f no
g <u>ordinary</u>
h <u>seldom</u>
i <u>request</u>
j <u>gigantic</u>
k <u>relaxed</u>

 Mathematics 2

a ¾ shaded, ¼ not shaded
b ¼ shaded, ¾ not shaded
c ½ shaded, ½ not shaded
d ⅓ shaded, ⅔ not shaded
e ⅜ shaded, ⅝ not shaded
f ⅖ shaded, ⅗ not shaded
g ⅝ shaded, ⅜ not shaded
h ⁷⁄₁₀ shaded, ³⁄₁₀ not shaded

i 3
j 7
k 8
l 9
m 4
n 12
o 9
p 7
q 7
r 8
s 105
t 57
u 180
v 228
w 180
x 424
y 360
z 846

 Language Skills 2

a It is impossible to climb this cliff.
b There is a lot of nonsense in this book.
c Terry says he dislikes cabbage.
d The answer you gave me is incorrect.
e The price of the car is unreasonable.
f <u>fell</u>, <u>opened</u>, <u>blew</u>, <u>dragged</u>, <u>sat</u>, <u>slid</u>, <u>forgotten</u>, <u>plunged</u>, <u>thrown</u>, <u>scrambled</u>, <u>shivering</u>, <u>chattering</u>.

 Science 2

The food we <u>**eat**</u> has to be broken down so that it can be used by all parts of the body. We take food into our <u>**mouth**</u>. We chew it with our grinding <u>**teeth**</u>. A liquid called saliva mixes with our <u>**food**</u>. The saliva makes the food easy to <u>**swallow**</u>. The food goes down a tube to the <u>**stomach**</u>. In the stomach other <u>**juices**</u> mix with the food. When it is almost a liquid, the food goes into the <u>**small**</u> intestine. There it is <u>**mixed**</u> with other juices. Then it is ready to be used in all parts of the <u>**body**</u>. The food has been made into tiny <u>**pieces**</u>. It goes into the blood and is used as <u>**energy**</u> in all parts of the body. Some of the food cannot be <u>**used**</u> by the body. This <u>**waste**</u> food passes through the <u>**large**</u> intestine and out of the body.

Writing 2

a Harry is playing with a toy crane.

b The girls are making costumes for the play.

c Sara and Owen have measles.

d It is Spring and the trees are in bud.

e They cannot find the lost ball in the bushes.

f Thousands of years ago there was no money. Instead, people traded by exchanging goods. Later, people began using different kinds of money, like shells and flat stones with holes in them.
Some of these strange coins, as in the South Sea Islands, were as much as three metres across. Then, in time, people began to make money. Metal, which had always been considered valuable, lasted much longer. The Greeks were the first to make silver coins, with heads and symbols on them, very like the coins of today.

Thinking 2

a 2 uncles	b 2 aunts	c 3 cousins
d 3-6-1-4-5-2	e plum	f bench
g kind	h release	i scissors
j next	k shark	k slim

Reading and Vocabulary 3

There **was** a man who had five sons. These sons **were** always quarrelling **among** themselves. Their father decided to show them how **silly** they were. He collected five sticks, each the same length, and tied them **together**. Then he said to his sons, "Listen to me! Break this bundle of sticks over your **knee**."

"Easy!" said the eldest **son**. He took the bundle and **pulled** it against his knee with all his **strength**. But he could not **break** the five sticks in the bundle. Then each brother in turn tried, but the bundle remained **unbroken**.

"Let me show you," said their father, "how it can be **done**". He **untied** the rope which held the sticks together. Then he handed one stick to each of his **five** sons. "Now," he ordered, "each of you break the **stick** in your hands." The sons did so. Each stick **cracked** easily. "What do you **make** of that?" their father asked them.

His sons looked **puzzled,** and made no answer. Their father **sighed**.

"Don't you see?" he **explained** patiently. "When a man stands **alone,** he can be broken as easily as **one** of those sticks. But when a man stands **united** with others, nothing can break him."

Then the sons **understood** what their father had been trying to tell them. They become **ashamed** of the quarrelling they had done. The eldest son said, "I see – **united** we stand, divided we fall."

Mathematics 3

a I m	b table	c no	d yes
e 0.5 m	f I m	g yes	h 0.7 m
i radiator	j 179	k 189	l 189
m 79	n 268	o 88	p 277
q 198	r 228	s 445	t 959
u 2352	v 3087		

Language Skills 3

a If you want to **buy** flowers, you will find them **by** the vegetables in the supermarket.

b Stand over **here** by the window, and you will **hear** the waves on the shore.

c It's **too** cloudy **to** see the comet this evening.

d You'll **be** stung by that **bee** if you're not careful.

e That cut on your **heel** will **heal** in about a week.

f verb	g noun	h noun
i verb	j noun	k noun
l verb	m verb	n noun
o verb	p noun	q noun
r noun	s verb	t noun

Science 3

a oxygen	b dust
c the lungs	d blood vessels
e oxygen	f to a large vein
g to the heart	h the heart

Writing 3

a Sam's clothes were scattered all round his room.

b The baby's face is covered in porridge.

c The striker's shot was blocked by the goalkeeper's legs.

d The force of Ann's service knocked the racket from her opponent's hand.

e The lion's roar made the hunter's hair stand on end.

f On Saturday the morning was fine and warm. We drove to Hastings, parked the car and walked to the beach. The heavens opened. We were soaked!

g We've been waiting far too long. Isn't it time we gave them another ring?

h Don't just stand there! Do you expect me to move this piano on my own?

i I'm going camping in the Lake District with Tim and Jane. If you're coming you'll need strong boots, a change of clothes, a waterproof coat and a sleeping bag.

Thinking 3

a Birds of a feather flock together.

b A stitch in time saves nine.

c Two heads are better than one.

d theatre	e thermometer	f thirty
g handlebars	h foal	i stream
j MEET ME AT MIDNIGHT		

Sir Clotton was not a <u>very</u> brave knight. He did not like <u>fighting</u>. His servants spent <u>hours</u> dressing him in all his <u>armour</u>. When he had to fight, he used the longest <u>lance</u> he could find. One day he had to set out to fight the Black <u>Knight</u>. He <u>wore</u> all the heavy armour he could find. They had to use a <u>crane</u> to hoist him on to his horse. At last he was <u>ready</u> for the battle. Sir Clotton met the Black Knight at the edge of the <u>forest</u>. His opponent was a <u>terrifying</u> sight. Sir Clotton was so <u>frightened</u> that he dropped his lance and fled. He <u>decided</u> to head for the village, where he thought he might <u>hide</u>. But the Black Knight was close <u>behind</u> him. In the village Sir Clotton spotted an <u>empty</u> well. He <u>dismounted</u> and jumped into the well. Sir Clotton <u>stayed</u> down the well until the villagers told him that the Black Knight had <u>gone</u> away. Then a rope was <u>lowered</u> down the well. The villagers pulled and pulled, but Sir Clotton and his armour were too <u>heavy</u> for them. Finally, he was <u>hoisted</u> out with a crane, and he slunk away in disgrace.

a terrifying   **b** lance

c decided   **d** armour

 Mathematics 4

a 121   **b** 212   **c** 231   **d** 342

e 214   **f** 123   **g** 228   **h** 416

i

	1 thousand	1 hundred	1 ten
more	2758	1858	1768
start number ➡	1758	1758	1758
less	758	1658	1748

j

	1 thousand	1 hundred	1 ten
more	3098	2198	2108
start number ➡	2098	2098	2098
less	1098	1998	2088

k 4700   **l** 3682   **m** 5450   **n** 7920

o 6397   **p** 3799   **q** 6430   **r** 6983

s 7999   **t** 9029

Language Skills 4

a 14   **b** 7   **c** 1   **d** 3

e 17   **f** 10   **g** 3   **h** 8

i 2   **j** 5   **k** 7   **l** 5

m 9   **n** 17   **o** 7   **p** 10

q 7   **r** 7   **s** 5   **t** 1

u 9 or 10   **v** 4   **w** 2   **x** 4

y 6   **z** 8

Science 4

a inside   **b** skull   **c** lungs   **d** bones

e grows   **f** 200   **g** joint   **h** movable

i elbow   **j** cannot   **k** fixed   **l** centre

m blood   **n** bone   **o** marrow   **p** new

 Writing 4

a The Dunnes were eating their lunch.

"I've never seen such rain," said Mr Dunne.

"Listen!" said Lucy. "What's all that shouting about?"

Sam ran to the window.

"Wow!' he gasped "The road is covered with water!"

Mr Dunne opened the window. He saw a man wading along with his trousers held up.

Mr Dunne shouted to him, "What has happened?"

"It's the dam," shouted the man. "It's cracked. The water's flowing through."

"Look!" called Lucy. "The water's coming in under the door!"

"Quick, Sam!" shouted Mr Dunne. "The dinghy! Let's get it out!"

Sam and his father waded to the boat-house.

 Thinking 4

a 1 The farmer ferried the lamb across.

   2 He rowed back alone.

   3 The farmer ferried the cabbage/wolf across.

   4 He rowed back with the lamb and put it ashore.

   5 Then he ferried the wolf/cabbage across.

   6 He rowed back alone.

   7 The farmer ferried the lamb across.

b I   **c** M

d M   **e** X, W

f 6, 2   **g** 5p, 20p

h £2   **i** 11

 Reading and Vocabulary 5

Most of the bees do not set out in search of nectar until they receive <u>information</u> from the <u>scout</u> bees. The scout bees set out at <u>sunrise</u>. They search for a good supply of <u>nectar</u>. When a scout bee returns to the hive, the bees <u>crowd</u> round it. When the bees pick up the <u>odour</u> of the flowers, the nectar has been found <u>near</u> to the hive. A scout bee tells about the nectar <u>far</u> away by <u>dancing</u> around, tracing a <u>pattern</u> as it dances. If there is plenty of nectar, the scout bee gives the information by <u>vigorous</u> wagging of its <u>rear</u>. Slow <u>wagging</u> means there is a <u>small</u> supply of nectar.

 Mathematics 5

a £7·70   **b** £12   **c** £10

d £8·10   **e** £52·90   **f** 90 18 99 45

Use the picture to answer the questions.

a Is the height of the bookshelves closer to 1 m or 2 m? _____

b Which is taller, the table or the radiator? _____

c Is the height of the room more than the heights of the window and the door added together? _____

d Is the TV set taller than the radiator? _____

e What is the difference in height between the door and the window? _____

f Is the height of the TV set closer to 1 m or 2 m? _____

g If you placed the TV set on the table, would they together be taller than the door? _____

h How much higher is the room than the door? _____

i Which is the shortest object in the picture? _____

Write your answer to each subtraction on the dotted line.

j
```
  567
- 388
```
....

k
```
  867
- 678
```
....

l
```
  756
- 567
```
....

m
```
  768
- 689
```
....

n
```
  532
- 264
```
....

o
```
  382
- 294
```
....

p
```
  666
- 389
```
....

q
```
  987
- 789
```
....

Write your answer to each multiplication sum on the dotted line.

r
```
  38
x  6
```
....

s
```
  89
x  5
```
....

t
```
 137
x   7
```
....

u
```
 294
x   8
```
....

v
```
 343
x   9
```
....

Language Skills 3

Some words sound alike, but have different spellings and different meanings. Choose the correct word from the brackets to fill in the blank in each sentence.

a If you want to _____ flowers, you will find them _____ the vegetables in the supermarket. **[by/buy]**

b Stand over _____ by the window, and you will _____ the waves on the shore. **[here, hear]**

c It's _____ cloudy _____ see the comet this evening. **[too, to]**

d You'll _____ stung by that _____ if you're not careful. **[bee, be]**

e That cut on your _____ will _____ in about a week. **[heal, heel]**

Say whether each underlined word is a noun or a verb. Write the answer.

         f   **g**   **h**
Tony <u>kicked</u> the <u>ball</u> back to the <u>goalkeeper</u>.

        i   **j**   **k**
The storm <u>blew</u> the roof of the <u>shed</u> on to the <u>road</u>.

        l   **m**   **n**
The wolf <u>huffed</u> and <u>puffed</u> but the <u>house</u> stood firm.

      o   **p**   **q**
They <u>toured</u> the <u>islands</u> off the west coast of <u>Scotland</u>.

    r   **s**   **t**
<u>Yasmin</u> is <u>planting</u> a plum tree in her <u>garden</u>.

f _____
g _____
h _____
i _____
j _____
k _____
l _____
m _____
n _____
o _____
p _____
q _____
r _____
s _____
t _____

Schofield & Sims **Homework 4 Photocopiable Edition**

Read the passage and answer the questions.

Our bodies need oxygen. We get the gas oxygen from the air we breathe. When we breathe through the nose, the hairs in the nose stop dust going into the body. The air is warmed in the nose. It passes through the throat, down the windpipe and into the lungs. There is a lining of tiny blood vessels in the lungs. Oxygen from the air is taken into these blood vessels. The gases that are not needed from the air are then breathed out of the body.

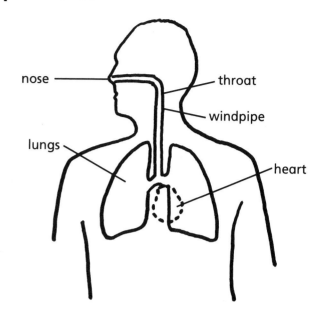

The blood vessels carry the oxygen to a large vein. In this vein the oxygen is carried to the heart. The heart then pumps the blood with oxygen to all parts of the body. Without this supply of oxygen, the body cannot live. The pipeline of blood vessels in the body is about 97,000 kilometres long.

a Which gas does our body need? _____

b What do hairs in the nose stop from getting into the body? _____

c Where does the air go from the windpipe? _____

d What lines the lungs? _____

e What do the blood vessels take from the air? _____

f Where do the blood vessels carry the oxygen? _____

g Where does the large vein carry the oxygen? _____

h What pumps the oxygen to all parts of the body? _____

Writing 3

An apostrophe ' is used to show the owner of something.
The apostrophe is added to the noun naming the owner, and this is usually followed by an 's':

the mother of Sandra = Sandra's mother.

Put apostrophes in the sentences below.

a Sams clothes are scattered all round his room.

b The babys face is covered in porridge.

c The strikers shot was blocked by the goalkeepers legs.

d The force of Anns service knocked the racket from her opponents hand.

e The lions roar made the hunters hair stand on end.

Punctuate the following sentences.

f on saturday the morning was fine and warm we drove to hastings parked the car and walked to the beach the heavens opened we were soaked

_____

_____

_____

g weve been waiting far too long isnt it time we gave them another ring

_____

_____

h dont just stand there do you expect me to move this piano on my own

_____

_____

i im going camping in the lake district with tim and jane if youre coming youll need strong boots a change of clothes a waterproof coat and a sleeping bag

_____

_____

_____

 Schofield & Sims · Homework 4 Photocopiable Edition

Here are three wise sayings or proverbs.
Find out what each one is and write it on the line.

a of   f 2 + gether

---

b A in   5 + 4 =

---

c 3 – 1 = r  9 – 8 =

Write the word from the brackets that fits each blank.

d Film is to cinema as play is to _____ .
[stadium, theatre, studio, church]

e Clock is to time as _____ is to temperature.
[speedometer, barometer, thermometer, gasometer]

f Ten is to twenty as fifteen is to _____ .
[thirty-five, forty, twenty-five, thirty]

g Steering wheel is to car as _____ are to bicycle.
[pedals, crossbar, saddle, handlebars]

h Cow is to calf as horse is to _____ .
[foal, cub, mare, stallion]

i Mountain is to hill as river is to _____ .
[sea, stream, lake, pond]

---

j Decode this message using the clue and write it down.

Clue: 3 1 18 18 15 20 = C A R R O T

Message:

13 5 5 20   13 5   1 20   13 9 4 14 9 7 8 20

Reading and Vocabulary 4

Fill in the blanks with words from the list. Use each word only once.

heavy	hide	wore	hours	hoisted
forest	gone	crane	empty	lance
very	ready	decided	terrifying	lowered
fighting	behind	armour	Knight	frightened
dismounted	stayed			

Sir Clotton was not a _____ brave knight. He did not like _____.

His servants spent _____ dressing him in all his _____ . When he

had to fight, he used the longest _____ he could find.

One day he had to set out to fight the Black _____ . He _____

all the heavy armour he could find. They had to use a _____ to hoist

him on to his horse. At last he was _____ for the battle.

Sir Clotton met the Black Knight at the edge of the _____ . His

opponent was a _____ sight. Sir Clotton was so _____ that he

dropped his lance and fled. He _____ to head for the village, where

he thought he might _____ . But the Black Knight was close

_____ him. In the village Sir Clotton spotted an _____ well. He

_____ and jumped into the well. Sir Clotton _____ down the

well until the villagers told him that the Black Knight had _____ away.

Then a rope was _____ down the well. The villagers pulled and pulled,

but Sir Clotton and his armour were too _____ for them. Finally, he

was _____ out with a crane, and he slunk away in disgrace.

Write the words from the story with these meanings.

a frightening _____   **b** a long spear _____

c made up one's mind _____

d protective covering worn in battle _____

Schofield & Sims **Homework 4 Photocopiable Edition**

In these division sums write your answer above the line.

a
```
      121
 3 ) 363
    - 3
    ────
      06
    - 6
    ────
      03
    - 3
```

b
```
 4 ) 848
```

c
```
 3 ) 693
```

d
```
 2 ) 684
```

e
```
 3 ) 642
```

f
```
 4 ) 492
```

g
```
 3 ) 684
```

h
```
 2 ) 832
```

Fill in the blank spaces.

i

	I thousand	I hundred	I ten
more	2758		
start number ➡	1758	1758	1758
less			

j

	I thousand	I hundred	I ten
more			
start number ➡	2098	2098	2098
less			

Subtract 80 from each of these numbers.

k 4780   **l** 3762   **m** 5530   **n** 8000   **o** 6477

_____   _____   _____   _____   _____

Add 90 to each of these numbers.

p 3709   **q** 6340   **r** 6893   **s** 7909   **t** 8939

_____   _____   _____   _____   _____

Language Skills 4

Most encyclopedias are in a number of volumes. When you want some information on a topic, you must choose the right volume.
The encyclopedia below is arranged alphabetically.

S&S ENCYCLOPEDIA																	
A-Bl	Bo-Cl	Co-D	E-Fr	Fu-G	H-In	Io-K	L-Mh	Mi-No	Nu-O	P-Q	R-Sk	Si-St	Su-T	U-Vi	Vi-W	X-Z	Index
1	2	3	4	5	6	7	8	9	10	11	12	13	14	15	16	17	18

You want information about Vampires. Entries beginning with the letters **Va** are in Volume 15.   *Answer:* Vampires – 15

In which volumes would you find the main articles on these subjects?

a Tiger _____   **b** Italy _____   **c** Apple _____

d Comet _____   **e** Yacht _____   **f** Octopus _____

g Diamond _____   **h** Mexico _____   **i** Carrot _____

j Gold _____   **k** Japan _____   **l** Guitar _____

m Moths _____   **n** Yoghurt _____   **o** Ireland _____

Some encyclopedias, instead of being arranged alphabetically, deal with one broad subject area in each volume.

When you want information on a topic, you must decide under which broad subject it is likely to be found.

Volume 1	The Earth and Space
Volume 2	Mankind
Volume 3	Animals
Volume 4	Plants
Volume 5	Countries of the World
Volume 6	Famous People
Volume 7	Transport and Communication
Volume 8	Work and Industry
Volume 9	The Arts
Volume 10	Sport and Entertainment

In which volumes would you probably find the main articles on these topics?

p Skiing _____   **q** Railways _____   **r** Computers _____

s Russia _____   **t** the Moon _____   **u** Theatre _____

v Oak _____   **w** Cavemen _____   **x** Strawberry _____

y Winston Churchill _____   **z** Supermarket _____

Schofield & Sims   **Homework 4 Photocopiable Edition**

After each section there are two words in brackets.
Write the correct word in the blank in the sentence.

a The skeleton is a frame of bones that supports the body. It protects the organs _____ the body. **[outside, inside]**

b The bones of the _____ protect the brain. **[skull, neck]**

c The ribs protect the heart and _____ . **[lungs, stomach]**

d The skeleton of a baby has about 350 _____ . **[organs, bones]**

e As the baby _____ , some of the bones join together. **[moves, grows]**

f An adult skeleton has about _____ bones. **[400, 200]**

g The place where bones meet is called a _____ . **[split, joint]**

h There are _____ joints, which allow movement. **[rigid, movable]**

i The joints at the knee, _____ and shoulder are movable joints. **[elbow, ribs]**

j Then there are fixed joints, where the bones that meet _____ move separately. **[cannot, can]**

k Most of the bones in the skull meet in _____ joints. **[movable, fixed]**

l Some bones have a soft _____ , called bone marrow. **[outside, centre]**

m Bone marrow takes matter from the _____ and puts it into the bone. **[blood, bone]**

n This keeps the _____ healthy. **[bone, blood]**

o Bone _____ also helps to make new blood. **[matter, marrow]**

p The _____ blood joins the bloodstream in the body. **[new, old]**

Dialogue (exact words spoken) is placed inside quotation marks:

"Are you listening?"

The dialogue is also separated from the rest of the sentence by a comma, a question mark or an exclamation mark.

When using quotation marks, a new line is started for each new speaker. For example,

"What time is it?" asked Oliver.

"It's time you had a watch," replied Frank rudely.

Write the passage, including quotation marks and any missing punctuation.

The Dunnes were eating their lunch I've never seen such rain said Mr Dunne Listen said Lucy Whats all that shouting about Sam ran to the window Wow he gasped The road is covered with water Mr Dunne opened the window He saw a man wading along with his trousers held up Mr Dunne shouted to him What has happened Its the dam shouted the man Its cracked The waters flowing through Look called Lucy The waters coming in under the door Quick Sam said Mr Dunne The dinghy Lets get it out Sam and his father waded to the boat-house

_____

_____

_____

_____

_____

_____

_____

_____

A farmer had to cross a river to get to his home. With him he had a wolf, a lamb and a cabbage. On each crossing the boat would carry only one of them and himself. But he could not leave the wolf alone with the lamb. The wolf would kill the lamb. He could not leave the lamb alone with the cabbage. The lamb would eat the cabbage. How did he manage to get all three across the river?

The following is the answer to the farmer's problem, but some of the words have been left out. Write the correct words in the blanks.

a 1 The farmer ferried the lamb across.

2 He rowed back alone.

3 The farmer ferried the _____ across.

4 He rowed back with the _____ and put it ashore.

5 Then he ferried the _____ across.

6 He rowed back alone.

7 The farmer ferried the _____ across.

Fill in the blanks.

b A E __ O U

c Y S __ G A

d A D G J __ P

e A Z B Y C __ D __

f 12 10 8 __ 4 __

g 1p 2p ___ 10p ___ 50p

h £1 £1·50 _____ £2·50

i 1 2 4 7 __ 16 22

Read the passage.

As the day begins most of the bees remain in the hive. They do not simply fly about in any direction in the hope of finding flowers with plenty of nectar. They wait until they know just where these flowers are to be found.

The scout bees get this information. At sunrise about twelve of them set out. Most of them fly in ever-widening circles away from the hive, seeking places where nectar is in good supply.

When a scout finds some nectar it eats some to give it energy and flies straight back to the hive. The bees crowd round it, eager for the information that will enable them to begin a day's work.

If the nectar has been found near to the hive, the bees pick up the odour of the flowers and fly straight to the place. But if the scout has found the nectar far away, it tells the bees the kind of flowers that are open and their direction from the hive. The scout does this by dancing around, tracing a pattern which is understood by the other bees. As it dances, it wags its rear from side to side. Vigorous wagging is a sign that there is plenty of nectar, and it is the signal for most of the hive to fly to the place. But if the wagging is slow, then the other bees know that there is a small supply only, and many of them will wait for better news from one of the other scouts.

Complete the sentences by writing words from the passage in the blanks.

Most of the bees do not set out in search of nectar until they receive _____ from the _____ bees. The scout bees set out at _____ . They search for a good supply of _____ . When a scout bee returns to the hive, the bees _____ round it. When the bees pick up the _____ of the flowers, the nectar has been found _____ to the hive. A scout bee tells about the nectar _____ away by _____ around, tracing a _____ as it dances.

If there is plenty of nectar, the scout bee gives the information by _____ wagging of its _____ . Slow _____ means there is a _____ supply of nectar.

FISH AND CHIPS £1·80

HAMBURGER £1·20

CHICKEN AND CHIPS £1·50

JACKET POTATO WITH CHEESE 90p

MUSHY PEAS 20p

a On the way back from the seaside Mum and Dad were too tired to cook a meal. So they said we would have a take-away. Mum and Dad went for fish and chips, and I wanted chicken and chips with mushy peas. The twins both wanted a hamburger each. What did the take-away cost?

Total cost _____

b How much would 5 hamburgers and 4 chicken and chips cost?

Total cost _____

c How much would 5 fish and chips with mushy peas cost?

Total cost _____

d How much would 5 jacket potatoes with cheese and 3 hamburgers cost?

Total cost _____

e A coach stopped off at the take-away and the shop was given this order.

  10 fish and chips
  5 fish and chips and mushy peas
  8 hamburgers
  6 chicken and chips
  7 jacket potatoes with cheese
What is the total cost?

Total cost _____

f **Circle all the numbers that are multiples of 9.**

  90   28   18   99   33   79   23   19   45

Schofield & Sims
HELPING CHILDREN TO LEARN

Schofield & Sims was established in 1901 by two headmasters and since then our name has been synonymous with educationally sound texts and teaching materials. Our mission is to publish products which are:

- Educationally sound • Good value • Written by experienced teachers
- Extensively used in schools, nurseries and play groups
- Used by parents to support their children's learning

HOMEWORK 4

Exercises in reading and vocabulary, language skills, writing, mathematics, science and thinking. Suitable for use at home, with or without parental help. Each book includes an answer booklet.

Homework Book 1 - 0 7217 0845 5   **Homework Book 3 -** 0 7217 0851 X

Homework Book 2 - 0 7217 0846 3   **Homework Book 4 -** 0 7217 0852 8

Author   Chris Burgess
Cover design   Curve Creative - Bradford

©1997 Schofield & Sims Ltd.

First printed 2003
Printed by Fulcrum Colour Printers, Ripponden

Information

For further information about products for pre-school, Key Stages 1 and 2, please request our catalogue or visit our website at **www.schofieldandsims.co.uk**

Schofield & Sims

Dogley Mill, Fenay Bridge, Huddersfield, HD8 0NQ
Phone 01484 607080   Fax 01484 606815

e-mail sales@schofieldandsims.co.uk

ISBN 0-7217-0968-0

9 780721 709680 >

Price £6.95
Key Stage 2
Age Range 7-11 years